# My Collage

## a collection

### of

### poems & writings

#### by
#### Neicey Writes

Neicey Writes Publishing, Wichita Falls, TX

*ISBN Paperback 979-8-9892875-0-5*
*ISBN eBook 979-8-9892875-1-2*
*Library of Congress Control Number: 2023917376*

*Neicey Writes Publishing*
*Wichita Falls, Texas*

# *Dedication*

*T*his is dedicated to my mother, Gail, who told me I was rich and needed to do something with it. So, here's to doing something with it. I love you always and forever ❤

# Table of Contents

~ 4 ~

~ 5~

# Introduction

O nce upon a time in a land far away...
This is how most fairy tales typically
start. However, this is not a fairy tale. Instead,
it is a "dream come true". It has been a dream
of mine to be a published author, and here is
the first of many future publications. My
prayer is that you enjoy reading it as much as
I enjoyed writing it

W ithin these pages you will find a collection of poems and writings that represent a beautiful collage of emotions. I believe what makes a collage so beautiful is the randomness of the size of the items, how the items are chosen, or the placement of said items. When I was brainstorming on how I wanted to present my heart, I knew I did not want to group, or categorize, the contents. What fun is that?

My desire is that as you read through the collage, you can relate to the joy & pain, love & loss, and hope & reflection.

*S* ometimes, it's nice to know a little bit about the artist, entertainer, author, or even the person presenting what is about to be experienced. With that said, I believe it would be fitting to let you know who I am, or at the very least who I think I am. LOL

## Who Am I

*Who am I? I'm me. Me is all I know to be.*

*I like to think I'm a strong black woman.*

*Let's not forget I'm only human.*

*Because as strong as I am, I do get weak.*

*But never weak enough to accept defeat.*

*It's when I'm at my weakest that my strength comes shining through.*

*Like when I have no income and all the bills are past due.*

*Of course, I may shed tears and cry.*

*Sometimes without a reason or why.*

*I cry, not only for obvious reasons, you see,*

*For me, crying is sometimes just a release.*

*As much as I cry, I laugh even more.*

Sometimes I laugh 'til my cheeks are sore.

I smile often because I've learned that it's my choice.

I've also heard it said that you can hear smiles in the voice.

I used to smile to hide the pain and hurts life brings.

But that only kept me from letting go of things.

And that in turn kept me afraid.

Afraid of loving and giving my heart.

Because when I love, I love hard.

Like many, I'm afraid of not knowing.

Not knowing which direction I should be going.

Or where the path I'm on will end.

Or if I'll fall in love again.

I rarely ever stress, I've been truly blessed.

I do get frustrated and angry too.

And that has a way of coming through.

I fuss at my little ones, and I might spank them too.

Sometimes the spanking is way overdue.

*I'm a fairly calm person,*

*Cool as the waters that flow in the creek.*

*I guess that's what makes me unique.*

*I enjoy being able to lift a spirit or two.*

*I encourage myself when I encourage you.*

*When others need a shoulder or even an ear,*

*I'm the one they call on when no one else is near.*

*I don't like to argue or have confrontations.*

*I'd rather solve the disagreement with simple communication.*

*You speak your mind. I'll speak mine.*

*Then, as mature adults, we should find a compromise.*

*To know me is to love me.*

*In loving me you'll find*

*All the love I have inside to give.*

*God is love. To love is divine.*

**y**es, God is love, yet He is so much more. For me, He is a healer, provider, protector, friend, the list goes on. What, or rather Who, do you think God is?

## God Is

When the day grows long and the nights are cold,

Remember God is always with us, His hand to hold.

When your heart is broken, in need of repair.

Remember God said He would always be there.

When the sadness seems too much to endure,

God said He would never leave you, of this you can be sure.

When the tears seem to be rivers flowing out to sea,

God said that your Comforter He would be.

God is master and creator of all,

It is only through Him we live and breathe.

He is always there to hear our call.

It is God who supplies our every need.

*I* 'm sure you have heard the saying "Big things come in small packages". One of the most powerful things in the world is only four letters.

## L–O–V–E

**L**ife is full of ups and downs, crazy curves and turn arounds.

**O**nly you can make the choice to be happy or sad, good or bad, forgive or stay mad.

**V**alue the time you spend with those you love. No one knows when they'll be called up above.

**E**very person has the right to give love and be loved in return. Love is the one thing most of us yearn.

*E*ven when we have love, there is always something more we want.

## What I Want Most

it frustrates me to know that

what i want most, i may never have.

even in my dreams it's never within my grasp.

it seems the closer i get to having it,

the harder it becomes to obtain.

it draws near when my attention is diverted.

it slowly creeps up as i move toward other goals.

i've covered myself with an invisible cloak,

hoping to hide myself from it.

yet, it tugs at the cloak and pulls at the strings of my heart.

how do i satisfy the longing to have it?

i return my focus in a desperate attempt to claim it.

but to no avail, once again i've failed.

it watches as my eyes begin to cry.

but it dare not comfort because then it must surrender.

it stands firm and the tears begin to dry.

it seems like forever since my first attempt to obtain it.

and i'm certain it'll be forever before i claim it.

it is hopeless to say the least.

what keeps me wanting it is unknown to me.

i understand now why they say...

people always want what they cannot have.

i may never have what i want most.

*H*ave you ever felt like something was missing but didn't know what it was? Then finally when that 'something' is no longer missing, you think to yourself, 'This is what I've been missing all along.'

## Craving Something Missing

*I have this craving that I can't seem*

*to satisfy.*

*A craving that goes beyond what's seen with the eye.*

*It goes past the taste buds and into the soul.*

*It brings all the senses together when it unfolds.*

*H*ave you ever been expecting to get something one way only to receive it in an unlikely package?

## Healing

*Often times I sit and think about how 'we' came to be. I think about how, at one time, we were mere acquaintances. Now, I love you endlessly. Of course, I noticed you from the start. I liked your style and offered my friendship. Now, you have my heart. I suppose I could have run the other way, never to look behind. Yet I needed to see if there was a possibility. Now, I know; you're mine. Ten days, I remember, that's how long it took when you made your feelings clear. "A lot has changed over the last 10 days," those were your words, my dear. Not believing this could possibly last, I tried to make sure you understood that you were free to walk when the time came. You chose to stay as we took it day by day. Since then, my life has never been the same. I fell in love with you before I knew what happened. Every day I fall deeper still. I love you more and more each passing moment. Now, I know what it takes for a broken heart to heal.*

*F or those of us who have been married, or currently married, do you remember how in love you were in the beginning? It seemed you just could not be apart for very long. Hourly phone calls just to "check-in and see what you're up to", constant "I love yous", all the fun you had, all the romance. You just could not get enough of each other, and no amount of affection was ever too much.*

## Never Too Much... Never Enough...

*I've told you day after day how I feel for you.*

*It's never too much to say, "I love you."*

*The time we spend making love, holding each other,*

*talking to one another, and just simply*

*being together enjoying the peace and quiet*

*keeps me praying that the day would never end.*

*It seems that there's just never enough time in the day to spend*

*showing you and telling you how I never want it to end.*

*So amazing you are to me.*

*I never thought I'd be blessed with a love so true.*

*And since you've become such a necessary part of my life,*

*I can't imagine my life without you.*

*In love with you always is where I intend to stay.*

*Here and now, always and forever, infinity and a day.*

*It's never too much to show you.*

*There are never enough words to tell you.*

*All the things I feel inside.*

*Just never stop loving me the way you do*

*because there's no way I could ever stop loving you.*

*I* believe when you are truly in love, you only have eyes for one and one only. You may even wonder, "How did I live life so long without you?" Whether it's your first love or fifth love, at that time they were the only one for you.

## Only You

Nobody can make me feel the way you do.

Only you can complete my thoughts the way you do.

No other has ever loved me with a love so strong.

Always by your side is where I belong.

No other arms can hold me as close.

Of all the loves that have come and gone, it's you that I've loved the most.

Never have I had kisses so sweet

until I was kissed by you and knocked off my feet.

You made me love you when I thought true love didn't exist.

You stole my heart with just one kiss.

*You're the only one who's in my thoughts every moment of the day.*

*In love with you for a lifetime is where I intend to stay.*

*For you am I inspired to write.*

*No other lips shall I kiss goodnight.*

*G*enerally speaking, we live life at a rather frantic pace. We hurry to work. After work, we race through the aisles of the grocery store frantically searching for the ingredients for tonight's dinner. We rush home after speeding through the drive-thru at the coffee shop. Dinner is quick and uneventful. Then it's off to bed only to do it all over again tomorrow. Can you remember the last genuine smile you gave, or even received?

## Something to Remember

What would you do if you lost your job today?

Would you get mad, cry, or make do?

Don't forget you have some bills to pay.

What would you do if you lost your home today?

Would you sleep in the car, in the park, or with friends or family?

If you have children, where would they stay?

What if, today, you lost your ability to talk?

Would you feel self-pity, misunderstood, or use pencil & pad?

How will you say "I'm sorry" if you couldn't talk?

What if, today you couldn't get out of bed?

What if you needed a care giver and needed to be fed?

There you would be with your all stripped away.

I'm sure this would be the time you would finally pray.

Wait. Did you thank Him when you started your new job?

When He gave you your home, did you thank God?

Are you mindful of the words you speak?

How many bruised emotions did you contribute to last week?

It's funny how we mistake the small things in life for mere occurrences.

Rarely stopping to think about the "what if's".

And take for granted our most precious gift.

Before it's all over and all is said and done,

Let us remember to give thanks.

*Because after all, He gave us His only Son.*

*S* ometimes the stresses of life itself can be a heavy weight on one's shoulders. Bills, kids, finances, and many obligations are thrust upon us, while some we took up on our own accord. How do we make it from one day to the next?

## A Day in Her Life

*Work is demanding.*

*The house is in turmoil.*

*Children are overly active.*

*Bills are past due.*

*Her body is tired,*

*and emotions are strained.*

*There are times when she feels like crying,*

*but the feelings are so intense*

*that the tears refuse to flow.*

*To no avail, she tries to devise a*

*temporary solution to her adversities.*

*Then finally she realizes there's only one solution.*

*So, she looks to Him with a sincere heart,*

*for He cares for her and promised to never forsake her.*

*Once again, she is at peace and able to face tomorrow.*

*M*any of us rely on our faith in God to get through the days of our lives. See what I did there? We attend weekly service. Some of us even attend the midweek service just for a little extra push to make it the rest of the week. Our pastors, priests, etcetera play a major role, if not the biggest role, in how we understand the doctrine of our chosen belief.

## Tribute to the Pastor

Jeremiah 3:15 declares that God will give us pastors according to His own heart.

In the first chapter of that same book, we know

that our Pastor was destined from the start.

He leads God's sheep, a good shepherd,

with a firm yet gentle hand.

And I've come to learn that he has no problem

letting you know just where and for Who he stands.

There have been times when I thought

no one would notice that my spirits were down.

However, as a good shepherd, he has often times given an encouraging word that would turn a frown upside down.

Our church family here is the most loving and caring people as many have said.

But I believe the reason that is, is not only because we want to let our light shine, but because of the Pastor by whom this church family is led.

Pastor, there are many wonderful things to be said about you.

And I pray that you would always know that we love you.

*H*ave you ever wanted to say something so badly that you thought you'd burst if you didn't say it? Have you ever given "the eye", or "the face", and no words needed to be spoken. I'm sure you have heard the saying "actions speak louder than words". Well, sometimes that's best.

## Unspoken Words

They often tell more than those we speak.

Sometimes we say things, and it's obvious

that there's much more behind the mere words.

We pick and choose our words carefully.

It's safer that way.

Afraid that if we say exactly what we feel,

the words may not come out right or be taken for granted.

Afraid even that somehow, I might jinx it.

Wanting to hear the words, say the words.

No, feel the words.

Why then are they unspoken?

Unspoken with the tongue, yes.

However, they're spoken through actions.

It's been said and proven time and time again that

"Actions speak louder than words".

So, until the time comes for the words to be spoken,

I'm content with the actions simply showing.

How then will I know when the time has come?

When the actions alone are no longer enough.

When the heart is filled and about to burst.

Unable to contain the words any longer.

When the words themselves make you stronger.

After you've done all you can do.

When nothing else will do.

Speak the words clear and true.

For then the words

will speak back to you.

**Y**ou ever find yourself repeating yourself? Sometimes you have to actually "repeat", but you have to find a different way to say what you just said so the other person can better understand what you're trying to say. Make sense? Well, these next two do just that.

## So Much More

I could come up with line after line trying

to explain the love I have for you.

We could listen to all the love songs ever sung,

or read all the poems ever written.

But what I feel for you is so much more.

So much more than mere prose could say.

And it grows even more with the passing of each day.

I've been in love with you for some time now,

and I'm falling deeper still.

Each day I wonder if it's possible to be

any more in love with you than I am already.

Each day I'm answered with a love that continues to grow steady.

# More Than That

Have you ever tried to count the stars in the sky? I love you more than that. Have you tried counting the grains of sand on the seashores? I love you so much more than that. Some might say that I love you so much it's a shame. Others might even say that love's a silly game. All I know is that if you asked me right now today, my answer would be "Yes!" Of that, I'm not ashamed.

You see it's not just the love we make, nor is it just the time we take. But it's all the little simple things you do. Like the way you pull me closer when I'm lying next to you. Or the way you keep me laughing when it's been a stressful day. Even when you let me know how you feel in your own special way. It's the little things you do 'just for me' that my love for you goes deeper than the deepest sea.

I could quote all the love songs ever sung, or all the poems ever written. None of them would come close to describing my love for you. I can't begin to tell you enough times just how madly in love I am with you.

G rowing up near the gulf, one thing we could always be sure of was that it was going to rain. I used to love sitting on the porch, or near an open window, enjoying the rain.

## Rain

*Your love refreshes me everyday*

*just as the rain refreshes the earth in it's own heavenly way.*

*My heart explodes with love for you*

*like the blooms burst open after the rains pass through.*

*My heart and soul drinks in the love you shower on me.*

*It's never a drenching rain that floods as it pours.*

*But it's a steady rain that keeps me craving for more.*

*It rained yesterday afternoon. It rained this morning, too.*

*Whenever it rains, I have visions of making love to you.*

*Showering kisses over your body as I explore you.*

*Taking you for a ride slow and steady with the rhythm of the rain.*

*Declaring my love for you as I call out your name.*

*Reaching our peak as the thunder rolls.*

*Basking in the love we share, feeling the joining of our souls.*

*Just as the earth needs the rain, I need your love.*

*And just like the rain, your love is from the heavens above.*

*P*erfect. Without flaws. No improvement needed. Just right. Is there really such a thing? Well, in order for something to be perfect there must first be an imperfection.

## A Perfect World

*In a perfect world, all our wishes, hopes, and dreams would come true. We'd have no heartache, pain, nor disappointments. No love would be lost. No friendship betrayed. But what then would we have to be thankful for? How could we be thankful for life's experiences? How could we know when we've been blessed so that we may give thanks? When would we say thank you for the good times if there were no bad ones? How could we appreciate the people who cross our paths if there were no reason for them to come our way? What reason would we have to be afraid, and thus, rejoice when we've overcome that fear? Yes, I do sometimes wish the world was perfect because I have many wishes, hopes, and dreams. I also know that I've been truly blessed. For that, I give God praise. And because the world is not perfect, when things don't happen as I wish, hope or dream, I am not amazed.*

*D*o you remember passing notes in class? Ahh, the infamous "do you like me? Check yes or no." Or the secret admirer's note telling you they think you're cute. Have you considered writing a note to your spouse, or to anyone? Really, you should try it.

## A Love Note

*"How do I love thee, let me count the ways."[1] That's what a great poet wrote.*

*I'm not a famous poet though, so I'll just leave you this simple note.*

*I don't know what the future holds. I don't know how many stars are in the sky.*

*I don't know all the names of the fish in the sea or all the birds that fly.*

*I do know that I'm in love with you for more reasons than one.*

*I fall deeper with each day that passes, with the rising and setting of the sun.*

*So, I hope that this, in some way, let's you know how I feel.*

*I also know without a doubt that what I feel is real.*

*1 Elizabeth Barrett Browning, Sonnets from the Portuguese – Sonnet 43*

*M*any times, in society we hear of best friends of opposite sexes falling in love and moving the friendship to the "next level". Have you ever thought how many of those "next level" relationships are still together? Did they live happily ever after? If not, are they still friends, do they hate each other's guts?

## Friends – Lovers – Friends

*As friends we enjoyed each other's company.*

*We laughed, shared stories, and rarely disagreed.*

*Time passed. We grew closer.*

*And before we knew what happened,*

*What had begun as a casual, no-strings-attached affair*

*Had turned into something neither of us could have foreseen.*

*As lovers, we remained friends.*

*Sharing our hopes, dreams, as well as our fears.*

*It was nearly impossible to imagine life without one another.*

*Even with all that we'd been through, we were going to be together for years.*

*But as with all good things, 'we' as lovers came to an end.*

*And although I will never love another the way I love you,*

*I'm content just knowing that we have remained friends.*

*I* *s there ever too much love? Can you say "I love you" too much? I think not. With that said, here's another love note.*

## I Love You

*My love for you reaches higher than the highest mountain. It flows deeper than the deepest ocean. The love I have for you journeys tirelessly through the thickest forest and across the widest desert. If someone would've told me that I'd one day love someone as much as I love you, I would've thought they were crazy and indeed certifiable. Yet, today, here I am totally and completely in love with you. Is it possible to love someone too much? I don't think so, as long as God is always First. Our relationship, our love, has been challenged on so many levels that many ordinary couples would have called it quits at this point. However, we're far from being an 'ordinary' couple. Everything about us, both separate and together, is 'extra'-ordinary. It's scary to think of how my life would be if I didn't have you. With all my heart, mind, body, and soul, I love you.*

*T* here has come a time in all our lives where we had to make a choice between emotion and logic. Our emotions, our heart wants to jump in the deep end and hope we at least float. Our mind and practicality remind us of the last time we jumped and sank to the bottom, and tells us do not jump in, sit on the edge and put your feet in, or better yet, grab a lounge chair, relax and watch the others jump in.

## Heart vs Logic

*What do you do when your heart and mind are pulling in two very different directions with equal intensity? When does one out-pull the other? Is it safe to just "ride the wave" and see where you end? Or do you make a decision based on logical, yet emotional, histories of where you've been? Does it hurt less to continue living in a dream rather than face the coldness of reality, the tangible? How can you continue when your mind questions the heart? What do you listen to when you can no longer discern whether it is the emotional voice of your heart or the logical voice of your mind? If you choose to follow your heart, how can you be sure that pain doesn't await you in the end? If you follow your mind, will the pain hurt less simply because you saw it coming? Should a* list of pros and cons be made for both the heart and mind? What do you do when it seems your faith has been tested beyond limits? There was a time when I used to wonder why some would spend years hoping, wishing, longing, loving, waiting for their dream to become reality. Well, now I know firsthand. Does the mind ever change the heart? Does the heart ever change the mind? The answers would depend on the person being asked the questions. As for me, I'll continue to follow my heart. Should pain greet me in the end, at least I'll know I was true to myself, true to my heart. Hoping, wishing, longing, loving, and waiting with no regrets. "Out of [the heart] flow the issues of life." (Proverbs 4:23)

*Y*ou know, sometimes people are like turtles, withdrawing into their shell at the first sign of trouble. However, we shouldn't reside completely in our shell like the hermit crab. At some point, we should break free of our shell and live life to the fullest.

## My Shell

my shell. my safe haven.

safe from heartache. safe from pain.

in my shell i'm in control. free to choose who comes and goes.

rather than being left open to enemies and foes.

many have tried to get past it, but few have succeeded

and even less are still inside.

it covers me during the storms,

and protects me when the wind blows.

"when will you come out," they ask.

the answer, "only heaven knows."

*E*verything has a beginning, a starting point if you will. Sometimes a new start is required after the initial course has been completed. Sort of like starting a new level, or a new chapter.

## How It Began (A New Start)

*For so long, I had been locked away inside the fortress I had built around myself, and around my heart. All the past hurts, pains, and heartaches had left me so wounded I couldn't see my way out. Not only could I not see, but I was too afraid to even open my eyes to flip the proverbial light switch. At one point I had actually come out. However, by the time I realized it was a mistake, it was too late. Beaten again. So, in I went, back into my protective shell. My shell acquired lots of cracks here and there from where people tried to get in. That required too much patchwork. So instead of letting them crack the shell so they could come in, I decided that no one would come in until I came out.*

*That proved to work best for me. If one tried to force their way in, or crack my shell, then I knew it wasn't meant for them to be close to* me. On the other hand, if they were willing to wait patiently, they'd see that in due time I'd come out on my own. Those select few are near and dear to my heart because they understand the struggles I've been through. They are also the few people who "keep it real". I can always count on them to tell me the truth, even when it hurts. Lots of things come in shells. It doesn't necessarily mean the shell has to be cracked from the outside. Some things have to struggle and crack the shell from the inside to get out. Like the baby chicks, or ducklings. Even the butterfly has to struggle from the inside to come out of its cocoon. It's the struggle that makes its wings strong enough to fly.

The last two years, I had been contemplating making a move out of the town I was in to start fresh. The only problem was that I had no idea where I would go, how I would get there, and what to do if, and when I got to wherever I was going. Then along came "Rita". Now I'm in a new city making a new start. I've also always believed that if any intimate relationship is going to have a fighting chance at surviving, it must first be founded on true friendship. I think the best couples are those who were friends first. So now, here I am in a new city, new start, and new love. Ain't life grand?

*It's amazing to be able to look back on past events and see God. To see how He worked things out and to see His hands in, and on, life's situations, I can only trust Him more knowing that He's working everything out for my good. The last five years have really taught me how to trust and depend more on God. Now that's not to say that I don't get frustrated, discouraged, disappointed, and whatever else because I do. I have my trying, as well as crying, times. However, through it all, God is always there.*

*H*ave you ever been dreaming and having the most wonderful time in the dream, only to be awakened by the alarm clock, or the urge to pee? How many of you are like me and try to go back to where you left off in the dream? No one? Just me?

## Awakened

At night when the stars shine bright,

Why does my heart long to be held tight.

On a beautiful sunny Saturday afternoon,

I can only wonder who'll be with me to see the rising of the moon.

I've had many dreams of how sweet love can be.

However, I still ask, "Is there a love somewhere for me?"

I've sang many songs that express one's true love.

I wonder if there's a love for me sent down from above.

Across a crowded room, our eyes locked as they met.

My mind and heart start to race as he takes the first step.

"Is it me he's coming for? What if he asks for a dance?"

Placing my hand in his, I decide to take a chance.

In his arms on the dance floor, I'm on cloud nine.

I wonder if fate would allow him to be all mine.

"Slow down," I tell myself, "This is just the first dance.

Gotta find out first if there's a hint of romance."

Time goes by, and we meet at the same place, same time.

It feels like déjà vu, I remember this rhyme.

Only, things are different now. There's a different closing line.

A warm gentle kiss lightly touches my cheek.

It's the rays from the sunlight awaking me from sleep.

S o, it is recommended that we brush our teeth (and tongue, it's amazing how many people don't) at least twice a day, in the morning and before bedtime. Let me just tell you, in case you didn't know, it is a very noticeable difference in morning breath. We'll know if you did the recommended bedtime brush. I'm just saying.

## Good Morning Kisses

muahhh... good morning, love.

the sight of you when i open my eyes

brings a sweet joy i can't describe.

to feel your arms pull me near

quickens the pounding of my heart; i'm certain you can hear it.

the sound of your voice whispering 'good morning'

and the soft 'i love you', too,

makes me the happiest woman alive

just being able to wake up next to you.

the simple kiss on my forehead

is as refreshing as the morning dew.

the soft kiss on my lips is sweeter,

still tasting of the love we made last night.

just the good morning kisses from you

make my whole day bright.

muahhh... good morning, love.

*A*ny journey for any length of time, or distance, begins with one step. The first step must be taken at some point. Otherwise, you stand still, remaining in the same position, or place, never going anywhere else. That is of course, until you take the first step.

## Step By Step

*Step by step, day by day,*

*We journeyed along a life-changing path.*

*With rocks, potholes, and detours,*

*At times, we had to take a few steps back.*

*There were a few who started*

*And abandoned the rest.*

*Perhaps it wasn't their time to take this test.*

*Together we have laughed, disagreed,*

*And yes, some have cried.*

*Now at the end of our journey,*

*Together, we stand side by side.*

*As we move forward on our journey,*

*Our paths will soon have to part.*

*Let us always keep the memories*
*And friendships within our hearts.*
*Let us strive to do and be our best*
*No matter what comes our way.*
*Let us continue our life-long journey,*
*Step by step, and day by day.*

*I* learned that grief is a very real thing, and it is different for everyone. However, everyone grieves at some point in their lives. We typically associate grief with the passing of a loved one. Did you know that when you break up with someone, or if you're separated from anything/anyone that has become a part of your life, like a job you've had for 20 years, you will go through the grieving process. Again, that process is different for everyone. Everyone processes grief differently.

## I Cried Last Night

last night i cried. you were not there to kiss my tears away.

i hugged my pillow tight. you were not there to hold me close.

nervous, i woke from a bad dream. you were not there to comfort me back to sleep.

made breakfast this morning. missed you because you weren't there to share pancakes.

lunch was quick and uneventful. you weren't around for a rendezvous in the park.

had pizza for dinner. no need for candles and wine because you weren't there.

started to read a book before bed. fantasies
rarely come true, so i listened to some jazz
instead.

you were not there to hold me close, so i
hugged my pillow tight.

you were not there to kiss my tears away when
i cried last night.

*I*'ve heard said that funerals and memorials are for the living. I believe it gives us an outlet to express some of the emotions and feelings that come with grief. Sometimes I write. Here are a few expressions. They have been edited to omit names to protect privacy.

## Rest Easy

Rest easy, sweet one. You worked long and hard. Even with a smile, you had to bear much sorrow.

Yes, we'll miss your smile and fun personality. But we'll live on in the hope of seeing you again on the other side of tomorrow.

For a thousand years is as a day to God and a day a thousand years. We rejoice in knowing you're resting now. You will shed no more tears.

Yes, we'll miss you and love you still, forever and always. We'll cherish those precious memories until the end of our days.

# When, Why, How

*When a loved one is taken from us, we often
wonder why. So many questions unanswered,
but it is God who decides. "Why so soon?" we
ask. "Why this day?" "How could you let this
happen?" "There's so much I wanted to say."
We know it's not our choice. We're not the ones
to decide. We can only hope and pray that
God's light became their guide. For we only
have one life to live. It's appointed once for
each to die. We should live our lives as best we
can, in hopes of meeting in the sky. Are we
perfect? No. There are times when we do fall.
Yet God is Love. Love sent His Son. And that
Love can save us all.*

# 32

*Thirty-two years. That's how long, until. Best
friends from day one. We've laughed, cried,
and grew together come rain, come sun.
There's not a day that goes by where I don't
reach for the phone to call, to share with you
life's recent events. Yes, we talked about it all.
Yes, there are times I just let the tears fall.
While it seemed everything happened so
suddenly, I know in my heart it was a part of
God's plan. While it still hurts, I take comfort in
knowing you had placed your life in His hands.*

*H*ave you ever not told a secret? I'm sure during your childhood you made a pinky-promise, crossed your heart and hoped to die; you'd stick a needle in your eye. LOL The things we so naïvely said as children.

## My Best Kept Secret

we've known one another for a while now.

it seems that every time you're near my heart goes crazy.

just to see you smile makes me smile inside.

we talk about everything and anything.

well, that is of course, except one topic.

and that, my heart has forbidden.

i long to be the woman of your dreams.

the woman who fulfills all your needs.

the one to greet you with a kiss at the end of the day.

and when things get rough, the one who makes it all ok.

how i wish to be the spark to the flame that lights your fire.

and my love the heat of your burning desire.

i wonder if fate will allow us to be more than just friends at best.

but until then i'll keep you as my friend, and my love my best kept secret.

*H*ave you ever heard someone say, "Oh that doesn't concern me", so they don't get involved in whatever the situation may be? I'm so grateful that people are not God.

## It Concerns Me

*Psalms 138:8 KJV "The Lord will perfect that which concerneth me: thy mercy, O Lord, endureth for ever: forsake not the works of thine own hands."*

*If it has anything to do with me, concerns me in any way, He will perfect it. Big things like the surgery I had a few years ago, God perfected it; I haven't carried an oxygen tank in over a year now. The daily things like providing for my family, keeping my babies safe. We're not homeless, hungry, nor naked. Even the seemingly small things like an earring! I noticed last night I was missing an earring. Only God knows how much the earrings mean to me. After searching last night and again this morning, I put on the one earring. As I was getting into the truck this morning to go to work, I saw it, just as pretty as you please, right there on the floor. My God, in all His awesomeness!!! He has in the past, He is right now today, and He will continue to perfect ANYTHING that concerns me!!! My God is an awesome God!!!!!*

*M*ulti-tasking takes practice. You have to focus on multiple things at once while not letting one task dominate your attention. Once that happens, something is bound to go awry. Here's a devotional I wrote during a time when my focus was being challenged.

## Stay Focused and Don't Doubt.

*Isaiah 26:3 KJV; Romans 1:16-17 KJV;*

*Matthew 14:30-31 KJV; Matthew 8:8, 13 KJV*

*Mark 9:17, 23-24, 29 KJV*

*The past six months have been quite challenging. It seems to have been just one thing after the other, from all sides, from all angles, physically, emotionally, financially, and spiritually. However, with each challenge, the Holy Spirit has reminded me to stay focused and don't doubt. Staying focused on God brings peace. Staying focused on Jesus keeps me from sinking in the ocean of challenges I'm facing. Staying focused on the Holy Spirit allows me to discern the subtle reminders and follow His guidance. Staying focused is not always easy when life has so* many distractions. And yes, the devil knows how to distract us. He hears when we tell others what our desires are, what we hope and dream for. When we lose focus, or our focus is split, it's easier to get distracted. Then Satan creeps in and presents us with an "image" of what we have been hoping for, or really really want. He wraps it all nice and neat, slaps a bow on it, and we hurry to grab it. But, because our focus has been split or lost, we never stop to confirm if this was truly a gift from God. We travel down a path of our choosing. Not the path God has lain out before us. Then there we are praising and thanking God, while God is watching and allowing us to "do what we want"; after all, He gave us free will. Then when sorrow comes with this "image" of what we thought we wanted, He reminds us "You never asked me if that came from me. You wanted it so badly, you just assumed. My blessings maketh rich and add no sorrow" Then we have to go back the way we came to get back to square one. We must stay focused, praying without ceasing, as we are to always pray, praying in the spirit, so that the Holy Spirit will make intercession for us when we ourselves don't know what to pray. The more we apply focus the easier it becomes. Does this mean we'll never get distracted, no. But it won't be so hard to regain our focus.

*Doubt, like distractions, can come when we least expect it. Does this mean we don't believe God's word is true? Not necessarily, but each of us is different. Where my faith may be strong with health issues, your faith may be strong with financial issues. We all have a weak spot. Even Abraham, who is noted as the father of faith, didn't think he and Sarah could really have a child in their old age. There are times when I feel unworthy. Not that I don't believe He can make my body whole and take away the aches and pains. But what if it's just not my time yet, or what if I'm still holding on to something that I should let go? These are all questions I've asked. Then I'm reminded of Deuteronomy 29:29 KJV "The secret things belong unto the Lord our God: but those things which are revealed belong unto us and to our children for ever, that we may do all the words of this law". Perhaps there are angels fighting the demons that try to hinder my answer from God. There are times when life's challenges are overwhelming, and I want to stop and quit and give up because it seems like a never-ending cycle. But then God sends me little reminders to let me know and see His love for me, like reducing library fines, or urging me to check the balance on a debit card. Lord, I believe, but help my unbelief. Prayer and fasting. Both fasting and prayer are personal between us and the father. As we develop our prayer life* and add fasting, our relationship will develop more; our spirit man will be stronger, while the flesh becomes weaker. Ultimately allowing us to stay focused through life's challenges and to overcome doubt and distractions.

*"H*ello, how are you?" *Do you respond
with the cookie-cut "Fine thank you.
How are you", but keep walking before the
person can respond? I mean why ask if you
really don't want to know? Going forward,
might I suggest that IF you ask, the very least
you can do is wait for a response.*

# I Can't Rightfully Complain

*I can't rightfully complain. That's my go-to
phrase when I don't want to acknowledge the
pain.*

*Pain in my body, joints, and pain in my heart.
Really, I hurt every day. Where should I start?*

*Start from the bottom and work up to the top?
Or perhaps from the head down to the toe
below?*

*Below the surface of calm runs a current of
ever-changing emotions, silently crying for
help amidst chaos and commotion.*

*Commotion and chaos no one can really see
because the calm surface hides the deepest part
of me.*

*Me, the sweet lady with the beautiful smile.
Trying to cope with my issues all the while.*

*While I take the journey learning to deal with all my hurt and the pain, please try to be understanding when I say, "I can't rightfully complain".*

*S* ometimes, matters of the heart can be difficult to put into words. When this happens, sometimes, just sometimes, words go unsaid, feelings are kept inside, emotions are buried, and tears are shed within.

# A Heart's Untold Secret

*why is it so hard to tell someone*

*how you really and truly feel?*

*could it be that what you*

*think you're feeling,*

*really isn't real?*

*maybe you*

*mistook a smile,*

*or was it a friendly kiss?*

*surely it couldn't be more*

*than these to have you*

*feeling like this.*

*did you stay*

*up late last*

*night*

hoping they

would call?

only to awake the

next mornin' and find

they hadn't called at all.

did you ever stop to ask

yourself if they feel the same?

it's very possible to get mixed-up

while playing the lovers/friends game.

so, if you have friend, and you think

you're in love, relax and bide

your time. because after

all, what is meant to

be, will be. and

with that, i'll

end this

rhyme.

*A*hh, the falling leaves of autumn. What a wonderful time of year! The beautiful colors of the changing leaves, the gentle breeze blowing as the sun sets, this is the golden time of days.

## Falling

*I was thinking of you when I started this. The words just wouldn't flow. So, I decided to just tell you how I feel. I'm sure you'd like to know. I don't really know how to explain it, but whenever you're around I can't stop smiling. My heart starts racing. Oh my goodness, am I falling? I feel like I'm falling faster than I should. I don't know if that's bad or good. I've also thought about all the possibilities. You know, me loving you and you loving me. As wonderful as the possibility may be, it can't hide reality. The reality that you are there, and I am here, doesn't carry much promise. Yes, I've heard that real love can conquer all, cover any distance. Can it bring us together? Tell me your wishes, and I'll tell you mine. Then we'll see where it goes, what happens in time.*

*I* use the calendar feature on my phone quite often, especially for doctor's appointments I don't want to miss or reschedule. Some people need the full-page planner books. What do you use to remember, or keep track of important dates?

## Did You Remember?

i was in the produce section at the grocer the other day. i smelled a scent that reminded me of someone. was it you? i was in the bookstore when i heard a familiar laugh, i turned and no one was there. could it have been you? i was driving on the boulevard when i spotted a car in the rearview mirror. it turned before i could stop. was it you? the phone was ringing when i walked in, it stopped just before i answered it. i wondered if it was you? we had a stupid argument last night, and some hurtful things were said. both of us with confused feelings. both feeling misled. now i'm hoping to see you tonight so that we can make things right. i'd truly hate for your last thoughts of me to be from a stupid fight. i was sitting in the ez-chair when i heard your key turn the lock. when i spotted the contents of the things you carried, i was even more in shock. you'd been to the grocer and bought some whipped cream. you also went to the bookstore and tried not to make a scene when the salesclerk asked if she could help just as you were pulling my favorite book off the shelf. it was you i spotted on the boulevard, you held a small box in your hand. you say you called but there was no answer, wanted to tell me not to make plans. you softly kiss the tears that fell from my eyes. i thought you had forgotten, but what a surprise!

**for all the days we wish they could remember.......anniversary, birthdays, first kiss, first date, first time, etc...

*S* *tory time... So, I have this neck pillow that my mom bought for me over 10 years ago. Over the years, there are approximately 10 days when I did not sleep with this pillow. There was this one night I couldn't find it and was almost to tears. Just as I had resolved to suck it up and be a big girl, my grandson came in all smiles holding my pillow. My world was set right. I gave him a big hug and kissed him good night. I was able to finally go to sleep. Whew, what a relief! LOL*

## At Night

*When I lay awake late at night, I feel your arms hold me tight.*

*As I inhale the smell of your fresh clean scent, I can't help but think you're heaven sent.*

*Sent to turn my grey skies blue and kiss away the pain,*

*You came along just when I thought that I could never love again.*

*As I lay in your arms, I tell you just how much you mean to me.*

*How I love the way you make me feel physically, mentally, and emotionally.*

~ 72 ~

*As you pull me closer to you, I hear you whisper in my ear*

*Just how much I mean to you and that you always want me near.*

*Near to your heart, near to your soul, keeping you warm when life is cold.*

*Then we share a kiss so passionate and deep,*

*Filled with love and desire, my heart takes a leap.*

*How could this not be meant? Yes, you must be heaven sent.*

*As I feel your arms hold me tight,*

*Now I can sleep through the night.*

*T* hose of you who are "pulse-checkers" when exercising, how do you feel emotionally when checking your pulse? Are you overcome with satisfaction confirming your heart rate has accelerated? Do you have a sense of accomplishment/pride? What goes through your mind exactly? Never thought about it? Might I suggest that the next time you stop for a pulse-check, take a mental note of your "emotional gauge" if you will.

## Beat of My Heart

It took me a long time to allow myself to love again beyond the love I have for my family and friends, beyond the love of God I have for my "neighbor". I've had my share of heartbreak true enough. As my heart beats, pumping blood so I may live, my heart beats out the rhythm of love that keeps me alive. I'd rather let love flow freely from my heart so I may live fully, than to keep love locked inside my heart growing cold and stony only to die.

*H*as there been a time in your life where an event or situation made you rethink your life's choices? I mean, what moment in time caused you to change, or "turn your life around"? For me, it was when I found out I was going to be a mother.

## M-I-S-S-I-O-N

**M**other - she's a mother who loves her children and everyone else's.

**I**lluminating - she brightens up any room she enters.

**S**aved - she believes Jesus is the son of God.

**S**anctified - she's set apart and lives the life she talks about

**I**ntegrity - she's honest and has strong moral principles.

**O**ptimistic - she is always hopeful about how things will turn out even in stressful situations.

**N**urturing - she cares for and helps in the development of others.

*D*id you know that trees breathe? Yep. They sure do. In fact, they inhale the carbon dioxide we exhale, and they exhale the oxygen that we inhale! How awesome! Take a moment and watch as the breeze flows through the leaves. What do you see?

## Praise & Worship

Let everything that has breath... Are you breathing? Then you still have a chance. Praise Him with the timbrel and dance. Did you come here expecting to see a show? Maybe we should put the offering plates near the do'. You see, you're all welcome, free admission because praise and worship shouldn't be a competition. I guess I really don't know what you came to do. But if you came to worship Him, let's do it in spirit and in truth.

*L* ife takes on a whole new meaning when others are dependent on you. Well, for some people that is true. Your children for instance are dependent on you when they are young, so you "live" for them in a sense. For those without children, have you discovered your "why" or "reason"?

## I Need You to Live

I need you to live

For my own selfish reasons, you see

Who else can I vent to when people start to bother me

I need you to live

You cannot be replaced

When I'm a little down, I need to see your smiling face

I need you to live

When emotions are raging and filled with noise

It all quiets down in the presence of your calming voice

I need you to live

*If only for the encouraging words you give to others*

*As if they are your sister or brother*

*I need you to live*

*Yes, I know I can talk to Jesus*

*He's a friend indeed*

*So, I talk to the Jesus in you*

*That's the Jesus I see*

*I need you to live*

**Deuteronomy 30:19 KJV**
*I call heaven and earth to record this day against you, that I have set before you life and death, blessing and cursing: therefore, choose life, that both thou and thy seed may live:*

**Proverbs 18:21 KJV**
*Death and life are in the power of the tongue: and they that love it shall eat the fruit thereof.*

*M*y son used to daydream in school. I imagine he played, or created, short movie scenes in his head. I've never really been a daydreamer. However, I love to replay memories that make me smile. Think of a recent memory that brings you joy.

## While Thinking of You

i heard this rhyme while i was thinking of you.

it was as if i had stepped into a dream come true.

you and i were as one as the sun came shining through

my windowpane that glistened from the morning dew.

there were flowers on the stand at the foot of the bed.

and along with a small box, there was a card that read,

"for all the love you've shown and continue to give,

my heart has found new meaning in the life i live.

no words can i say, no song can i sing,

to express the joy that loving you brings.

so, with these flowers and small gift, i send

my heart which overflows with a love that will never end."

*M*y job. My house. My car... My wife. My Husband. My children... My this, my that. Do you feel accomplished? Contentment? A sense of pride? And yes, we should feel a sense of pride in our accomplishments. After all, it's a mighty po' dog don't wag its own tail.

## His

There's something about him staking claim to what's his. He asks if it's his and each time you say yes. But it isn't until he claims it with that one simple word... 'my' or 'mine'... that you realize he no longer has to ask if it's his. He knows it's his. However, even though he knows it, and maybe it's just a 'man thing' he may still ask, 'whose is it?'

*D*escribe yourself in one word. Not a phrase, just one word. Kind of hard to do, right? Have you ever tried to describe a flavor, or a feeling, and just couldn't find words to do justice?

## I Do

*There are many words I could use to try and describe my love for you. I could tell you that you're the sunshine that brightens up my day. Or you're the moon that shines on me in my darkest hours. I could even tell you that I love you more today than I did yesterday, but not as much as I will tomorrow. But all these words you've heard many times before. So, what words can I say that will be different than before? How can I tell you that it's you I adore? What words can I say to express how much you mean to me, how I need you in my life? It still amazes me when I think of how we've come to love when love wasn't even a thought. I can't imagine how life would be without you. You have become such a necessary part of me. You're the melody to the song my heart sings, and the rhythm of its beat. You're the pep in my step and the dance in my feet. With all the words there are in the English language, there aren't enough to describe how much I love you. All I can say is I do. I do. I do.*

*I*f only I knew then what I know now, a few things may have been different. I probably would have still ended up where I am now. Just maybe I would have seen some different scenery. You know, like when your GPS gives you different routes to get to the same destination. To toll or not to toll. LOL

## If Only You Knew

Look at you. Standing there all tasty and sweet.

Bet you have all the ladies offering you "treats".

Yes, we're friends, but my oh my.

If you only knew... I'm just too shy.

If you only knew how I dream of being your one and only.

Long sleepless nights would no longer be lonely.

When I talk to you after having a bad day,

I only wish to be in your arms and make it all go away.

When things are great and I'm feeling grand,

*I only wish that you could share it with me.*

*Me as your woman and you as my man.*

*Just to be the one to love you completely.*

*To shower you with kisses ever so sweetly.*

*For you to feel all the passion I have inside.*

*Just to be free with you, no longer having to hide.*

*Sure, it's just a dream, and some dreams come true.*

*Perhaps this one will, if only you knew.*

*E* enie, meenie, miney, moe. Do I stay or do I go? How many rounds until I'm picked? Fiddle-dum fiddle-sticks.

## Can I Be The One...

...you're dreaming of as you lie there deep in sleep?

...your body longs for when it feels that sensual heat?

...you whisper "i love you" to softly in my ear?

...who comforts you and kisses away your tears?

...who greets you at the door after a long day?

...you take a second look at as you watch me walk away?

...you confide in with cares that trouble your heart?

...you're missing when we are apart?

...who puts that sparkle in your eye?

...you love and cherish until the day i die?

...can i be the one who plays the melody to the song your heart sings?

*...can i be the one who is your all and all, you know, your everything.*

S ome years ago, I was a bit jaded and didn't really trust my heart to love. I couldn't imagine ever finding the courage to let someone get close again.

## Love Hurts

Love hurts. Yet it also heals. Then there are those times when it's hard to tell if love is real. Could it be infatuation? Or is it just old-fashioned lust? It's not easy to be certain, especially when it's so difficult to trust. It seems the more I try to 'keep it simple', the more complicated things become. Sometimes I feel like giving up, saying 'It's over. I give up. I'm done.' 'Follow your heart.' I've heard it said many times. I've even said it a few times myself. How about 'Experience is a good teacher.'? Judging from all the lessons I've learned, I think I'll place my heart on the shelf. Perhaps it'll remain out of harm's way and avoid being broken. Perhaps I'll be able to ignore its desires if they remain unspoken. Instead, I'll apply the lessons I've learned. I'll ignore the things for which my heart yearns. It's no longer safe to believe in the 'happily ever after'. Instead, I'll have to be more logical in the things I go after. I've come to finally realize that I've been living in the hopes of a dream. Yes, I know some dreams do come true. This *just isn't one of them, so it seems. I also know, for what it's worth, that my heart's desires may never go away. But if it's up on the shelf, 'out of sight out of mind', isn't that what they say? Yes, love heals. But it hurts just as much. It is what it is. Such is life. Life is such.*

*H*ave you ever ordered something through the mail, and it seemed to take forever for the package to arrive? But oh my goodness when it's finally delivered!

## He Sent Me You

*I wanted a man who believed in God, not a saint, but one who knows that God is God.*

*...He sent me you*

*I wanted an honest man. How can I give my heart to someone I can't trust?*

*...He sent me you*

*He must be willing and able to love me as he loves himself. How can anyone love another if they don't first love themselves?*

*...He sent me you*

*Please, let him be taller than I am. I want to be able to look up to him and not down on him.*

*...He sent me you*

*I'd like for him to be older than I am. I just have a thing for older men.*

*...He sent me you*

*Dear God, let him know how to cook. If I get sick, he still has to eat.*

*...He sent me you*

*He should know how to clean. If I get sick, the house shouldn't turn into a pig sty.*

*...He sent me you*

*Please, oh please, I want a man that can sing. Music is the rhythm of love*

*...He sent me you*

*He should be capable. The size of his ship needs to be able to handle the motion in the ocean.*

*...He sent me you*

*I never thought the day would come when my every wish came true.*

*My heart, still bruised from past relationships, longed for someone who*

*Would softly kiss my tears away and turn my gray skies blue.*

*Before I knew what happened and just when I had given up on love,*

*...He sent me you*

*D*o you remember, when you were in school, the lost & found section that was usually in the front office? Man, some of the things you could find there! Mostly clothes, ranging from shoes to hats; you could literally find an entire outfit if needed with accessories to match. There would be textbooks, gadgets, you name it! You just never knew what you would find there.

## Lost & Found

when love is lost, the

pain is felt deep down inside.

at times the pain is so great,

it's amazing you're still alive.

you decide to search for love

again, never quite knowing

just where to begin and

just when you thought

all hope was

gone,

that special someone came along.

you continued your search, hoping
for love to be found. 'til finally
one day you realize, since the
day that special someone
arrived, a truer
and sweeter
love had
already
been
found.

*W*hat were you doing when the nation received news of the Twin Towers being hit? I was at work, in an office. A few years later, my youngest brother joined the United States Marine Corp right out of high school. During his service, he completed three tours to war zones in Iraq and Afghanistan. I am indeed blessed to still have my brother with me. My youngest son is now serving in the United States Army. Our family is filled with veterans who have served and some who are still serving. Let us not forget those who did not make it home.

## As We Remember

*Lives were taken at the whims of others.*

*Aunts, uncles, grandparents, and cousins.*

*Brothers, sisters, fathers and mothers.*

*The lives of millions were changed in an instant.*

*Broken families both near and distant.*

*Those who risked their lives to rescue someone else.*

*Those who were left to pick up*

*The broken pieces that were left.*

*Brave ones who now serve to protect OUR rights.*

*Brave ones who chose to serve so that*

*WE may sleep safely through the night.*

*As we go about our daily routines,*

*Let us not forget the tragedies we've seen.*

*Let us remember the lives that*

*Were shattered and those that were lost.*

*Let us forever be reminded that*

*Although this country is free,*

*NOTHING is without a cost.*

**D**id you ever watch the movie "La Bamba"? A great movie, you should watch if ever you have the opportunity.

## Lover's Dance

*I could go on and on about how happy I am with you. However, the fact of the matter is 'happy' doesn't come close to describing how I feel. Whenever you're near me, my heart starts to flutter like the butterflies that erupt every time we kiss. The slightest touch of your caress sends chills bolting through me like a lightning bolt that ignites the fire that burns with desire deep within. The sensuous warmth as you breathe soft kisses on my neck, or whisper 'I love you' in my ear, melts away any ounce of remaining control, melting my mind, heart, body, and soul. Lost in your embrace, my saving grace, I rest in your strength that brings us face to face. Tracing your lips, I taste you sweetly letting our tongues dance seductively. As the kiss deepens, so does your entrance. Our hearts beating their own love cadence. As we dance the lover's dance, we climb to higher heights. Together we reach our peak, shattering into a million little pieces. Floating slowly back to solid ground, still in your arms safe and sound. Can you still feel my heart pound?*

*M*y oldest son smiles a lot. As a teenager, he would smile while getting fussed at. Even now, if someone is attempting to argue with him, he just kind of smirks. He can be so annoying at times. LOL.

## I Smile

*I smile because I'm happy.*

*I smile even when I'm sad.*

*I smile because when I think of all I've been blessed with,*

*My issues no longer seem so bad.*

*I cry when I'm overwhelmed with joy.*

*I cry when my heart has been broken.*

*I cry when I need to release all the words that can't be spoken.*

*I laugh when I hear or see something funny.*

*I laugh even when it seems there's more month than there is money.*

*I laugh, although life sometimes seems dreadfully cold.*

I laugh because I read somewhere that it's good for the soul.

I frown when my clothes don't fit as they should.

I frown sometimes when I feel misunderstood.

I frown when things don't seem to go my way.

I frown sometimes when I don't know the right words to say.

I love because it's what makes the world go 'round.

I love because in my heart I don't want hate to abound.

I love because God first loved me.

I love because even with all my faults, He loves me unconditionally.

When you are afraid of something, you wish to never have to face it. There's a TV show that makes people face their fears, and the last one standing wins the prize. Well, it's a no for me. I mean if life brings me to a point where I have to then I just have to. Otherwise, no thank you.

## I Hate Snakes

I hate snakes! Long, short, skinny, or fat snakes are creepy; that's a fact. We found a snake in my daughter's room. Can you imagine trying to kill a snake with a broom? My heart was racing and beating fast. After hopping across the bed, I had him at last. Hooray! Hooray! The creepy snake is dead! The broom has been broken, but I smashed the snake's head.

So, I have an auntie who has a couple of favorite movies. I mean her all-time favorites. No matter the time or day, if she scrolls the TV guide and finds one of the movies playing, she is going to stop and watch the movie. Point. Blank. Period.

## Loving You

a stroll through the park, a picnic after dark

a love song for two, a night of making love to you

breakfast in bed, one another we fed

lunch rendezvous, an afternoon of making love to you

dinner and a movie, a jazz club too

soft music sets the mood, oh how i love making love to you

*Y*ou ever had a smile that just wouldn't fade? Like, no one, or nothing, could ruin your mood. Sort of like how chocolate makes you feel with that first bite.

# What You Do To Me

*I don't know exactly what it is that you do to me.*

*But whatever it is I like it. Or maybe I do know what it is,*

*just too afraid to say it.*

*The way you kiss me teasingly on my neck*

*sends chills through me.*

*When our tongues meet with*

*a promise of what's in store,*

*the fire inside collides with the chills.*

*The collision settles in that*

*secret place bringing forth a sweet mist.*

*As the honeysuckle is a beacon to the bees,*

*so is that secret place a beacon to your love.*

*Yearning for entrance, it's a welcoming place.*

Welcoming you with a soft,

warm spot to rest your head.

Offering a soothing massage to release the tension.

Then as you relax, you feel the mist turn to showers.

Shower after shower until you are ready to let go.

This is only a portion of what it is you do to me.

It's the way you let me know

what's on your mind or how you feel.

When you tell me something special

about who you are makes it real.

How you want to know, yet you never push.

You simply wait for the time when I choose to reveal

those small nuggets of me that keep me real.

It's the way my heart leaps whenever you arrive.

The smile you keep on my face, you're that sparkle in my eyes.

*So, whatever it is that you do to me,*

*just know that I like it.*

*Whatever it is that you do to me.*

*W*hat motivates you to be who you are? Who motivates you to do what you do? Why did you start on your current path? How many times have you wanted to quit? How many times did you quit? And finally, do you love who you are and what you do?

## You Are

You are the inspiration that makes me want to write.

You are the moon that shines on me at night.

You are the rhythm that beats within my heart.

You are the reason love was given a new start.

You are the balance that evens out my life.

You are the desire, that apple of my eye.

Never have I had a love so true.

Because of all that you are to me,

I'll never stop loving you.

When working on a team project,
someone has to take the lead.
Sometimes, no one wants to lead, while other
times, everyone wants to lead. It can be quite
the conundrum. There are times, however,
when the person that steps up to take the lead
is the ONE person everyone wishes would step
down LOL.

## Taking Charge

Why do I do what I do? Because... I love you
and am very much in love with you. For those
reasons alone would I cook your favorite meal
or do your laundry. Be mindful that you don't
take it for granted because there's someone out
there somewhere who would truly appreciate
it. Knowing that you're happy brings me
happiness. As your woman, it's my prerogative
to make you happy. Just as you, as my man,
want to be the one making me happy. You say
you love when and how I 'take charge'.
However, in my mind I don't see it as 'taking
charge'. I'm simply giving my man what I
know he loves. The response I get in return
makes me want to keep giving until one of us
gives up. When I take the 'top' position, it's not
because I want to be in control. But it allows
me to look in your eyes and see your soul. To
see the depth that love beholds. To see your

face as ecstasy unfolds. To ride with you to the clouds as we explode. Floating back to earth. Holding you close, I'll never let go.

*T*here was this dog in the neighborhood that had been struck by lightning. It seemed to have made the dog even fiercer than before. I remember this one afternoon I was riding my bike, and the teenage boy who owned the dog happened to be walking him, headed in my general direction. The dog somehow overpowered and started pulling the boy directly toward me! Gratefully, the dog was only able to attack my favorite pair of sneakers. I never liked that dog.

## Storms

*There are so many things I want to say. I don't know where to begin. Let me start by saying, 'I love you.' And I am very much in love with you. Turbulent emotions run wild as the winds of the storm increase. The rains begin to fall as life begins what seems to be a chaotic spiral of never-ending confusion. As the winds and the rains increase, they combine to wreak havoc tossing and drenching everything in their path. As the storm continues, it seems to hover above showing no signs of dissipating soon. We wonder and pray, 'Dear God, how long shall the storm last? How much longer will I have to endure?' No sooner than the prayer is finished we're reminded, 'He'll never put more on us than we can bear. And the race is given to* them that endure until the end.' With this, we pray for the strength to endure the chaos and confusion of the storm, of life. Just when we begin to think this storm may never end, the rains begin to slack, and the winds lessen. The storm is passing, and the sun slowly begins to peak from behind the clouds. Yet it is evident that there was a storm, for the damage it seemed to have caused is obvious. Life is left in an incomprehensible mess as it appears. What do we do now? Do we live life aimlessly amidst the debris and confusion? How can we move on with everything left in shambles? Where do we go from here? Piece by piece, bit by bit, step by step, and day by day – that is how we move on and go forward. Knowing this, we resolve to go on and move forward in life. We begin to pick up the pieces shattered by the storm. Mending that which can be repaired, discarding that which is of no use any longer, we begin to see some semblance of organization take form in a life turned upside down. As each day passes, we take steps to not only restore things as they were before, but to bring things to a new and improved state, a higher level. Finally, as we take joy in the accomplishment of our work, we must be sure to prepare and stay ready for the next storm because surely there will be another. We may not know when, or how strong, the next storm may be. But rest assured there will be another storm. They're a part of life. As the seasons prepare for change, they bring about storms. The storms help to prepare the earth for the upcoming season. Whether it is winter, spring, summer, or fall, there is a storm for all. For each season and each area of the earth, area of life, the storms are different, achieving very different results, yet necessary changes. Winter storms prepare the earth to bring forth its fruit in spring. Spring storms prepare the earth's atmosphere for the gloriously relentless heat of summer. Summer storms help to cool us as the earth prepares to rest while the hurricanes through summer and fall prepare the way for winter to return. The cycle is continuous just as the cycle of life. While we yet live, we will have storms to endure as we move from one phase, or chapter, of life to another. For some the storms will seem to be a greater trial than they are willing to go through. Others will struggle through their storms with bitterness in the end, while others will acknowledge the reason for the storms and grow stronger because of them making the most of the storms. Things work out best for those who make the best of the way things work out. We've weathered the storms thus far, in love. Because of them, our love has grown stronger than we ever could've imagined. Together, we'll continue to move through the storms coming out stronger in the *end with a love that continues to stand the tests of time. What more can I say, I love you.*

*I* used to LOVE LOVE LOVE coffee! Really, I could drink coffee any time of day or night. My grandmother once told me that coffee does whatever you want it to do. Whenever company arrived, she would put a pot of coffee on, no matter the hour. I never thought I'd ever be able to do without it.

## From the Heart (Madly)

It's hard to put into words the love I have for you.

It seems that whenever I try the words die, right on the tip of my tongue.

I kiss you instead.

As if the words would somehow flow from my tongue and seep into your soul, the kiss deepens, and passions unfold.

As I regain control of my senses, I try to steady the rate of my heart beat and find my feet.

I've never been in love like this before.

I'm constantly wanting more and more.

It's not enough to just tell you.

I want to show you.

*I need to show you.*

*But what is there for me to do that I haven't done already?*

*Is there a mountain I could climb, or an ocean I could swim?*

*I could serenade you with song after song, but that would last how long?*

*How long will this last, this love we share?*

*Always and forever, I pray.*

*I don't want to be without you, not even for a day.*

*I miss you terribly each moment you're away.*

*Kiss me again and whisper in my ear.*

*Tell me you love me, and you'll always be here.*

*Here, with me always, is where you belong.*

*Never have I known a love so strong.*

*So strong that it makes me weak from wanting you so badly.*

*Not only do I love you, but I'm in love with you madly.*

*M*y children would try to talk their way out of doing the dishes. "I washed dishes last night", "She hasn't washed dishes in two days", and "Why I gotta do the dishes all the time?" I don't recall ever whining about having to do dishes. I just did it. Being the oldest, I just didn't trust my brothers to do the job correctly.

## Why Me

*why did i have to fall for you so fast?*

*i knew from the start that this wouldn't last.*

*never stopping to think of the consequences,*

*i simply followed the urge of my senses.*

*just to smell the scent of your cologne,*

*or hear the sound of your voice with its deep rich tone,*

*the feel of your touch as you caress my skin,*

*not to mention the desire when you're deep within.*

*my senses left me wanting more.*

*more of what i'd been missing before.*

before you came along, it seems,

i only felt this way in my dreams.

now the time has come for you to leave

i stand, alone, wondering "why me".

*A* few months back, I upgraded my cell phone. Yes, I did! Finally, I now have a proper smartphone. I won't say which model I have, but I will say that I was 13 generations in phone years behind.

## Graduation

*So, you've moved from childhood to adulthood. Life up to this point has been all good.*

*Don't think so? Don't worry, you're about to experience a whole new life. It can still be all good if you've accepted Jesus Christ.*

*Not just as your Lord and Savior, but also as your friend. He'll stick closer than a brother and will be with you through the thick and the thin.*

*Dad, mom, even grandparents have trained you up in the way you should go. Don't hesitate to seek their wise counsel when you come to a "fork in the road".*

*Remember to acknowledge the Lord... in... ALL... your ways. Let Him direct your path because even as parents, we have "off" days.*

*No, we didn't take a day off from parenting. It's just that sometimes our emotions and* feelings may get the best us. This is why in GOD you should put ALL your trust.

I'll bring this writing to an end, lest I overextend myself. My prayer is that as you journey into adulthood, if you carry from your childhood nothing else, you understand that a closer relationship with God is the best gift you could give yourself.

*Who doesn't like a good crime show? Do you try to solve the crimes along with the actors? I'm not sure how true it is, but they say you can never truly get rid of all the blood. They always bring in that trusted UV light and find the smallest of traces!*

## Small Trace

*It's been a long time since I've seen your face.*

*Seems like forever since I've heard your voice.*

*Yet, in my heart there is still a small trace.*

*A small trace of hurt after making that choice.*

*The choice to love you even though I knew*

*That there could never truly be a 'Me & You'.*

*You needed someone to love you for you.*

*I needed someone to give my love to.*

*But there's much to be said for loving another.*

*Not just the love you have for your sister or brother.*

*But the love that causes you to forgive the unforgivable,*

*Reach for the unreachable and dream the impossible.*

*For with you, this is the love I had.*

*This is the love that many wish they had.*

*But time has passed, and things have changed.*

*And, yet still a small trace remains.*

*A small trace of the love that we once knew*

*When I made the choice to start loving you.*

*A*s a kid I loved, and still do love, Looney Tunes. Tweety Bird is my favorite. And the music/soundtrack is unforgettable. I was on hold once and the music playing was "Figaro". Who knew we were being groomed to love classical music through cartoons?

## Symphony

Life, like music, is a beautiful symphony. From beginning to end there are highs and lows. The music, like life, takes us through joy and pain, from relaxing to adventurous. We feel every emotion as the symphony tells life's story. However, we know that it will eventually come to an end. If we are fortunate, the symphony, like life, will leave us wanting more. One more stanza, one more day. While we're saddened that such a glorious symphony had to end, we will always have the memories of how we felt as we experienced each high and low, each swell and crescendo. We'll share how wonderfully orchestrated this life's symphony was played. Sweet melodies will linger in our memories. Each memory will hold a different tune as the symphony touched us all differently. Yet each of our lives has been enhanced having experienced even a small portion of this Symphony. We should hope that *our own life's symphony is so beautifully composed.*

*O* ver the years, I've had five surgeries. Regardless of the types of surgeries, there was one constant. Healing doesn't happen overnight. It takes time, patience, and a few pain killers. LOL

## A Process

*Because of you, I know my heart has mended. I no longer have to be afraid to love, and although careful of who receives, no longer afraid to open my heart, bare my soul for others to behold. It's amazing how things happen, and people change. I had gone through a storm. A cleansing, if you will. Material things thought dear to me, I found I didn't need them at all. Some whom I thought were friends, not friends at all. While letting go of all that, I've let go of a lot more. Past hurts, pains, insecurities. All washed away. Had you not come along, I would not have bothered to look inside hoping to let my heart be my guide. I've also come to realize something I've always known is that some things are just not meant to be regardless of how much we've grown. Instead of trying to figure out how to make a dream come true, I'll learn to be content with what I have, where I am, who I'm with, and who I am. Yet not satisfied, but always working to improve. And one day, when the* time is right, I'll wake up and realize that my dreams didn't have to be made. They simply happened because it is a process for me. And what's meant to be will be.

*I*t has been said that we should mourn the birth of a child and rejoice when transition is made from this life. Here are a couple poems that helped me celebrate.

## Don't Cry For Me

*Don't cry for me. I'm doing just fine.*

*You see, I had my ticket, and the train came right on time.*

*Yes, I've left this ol' earthly body. My physical presence, I know you're gonna miss.*

*If you get right with Jesus, it'll be the last time you see me like this.*

*The next time you see me, I'll have on a white robe.*

*I'll have a few wings, and a crown of jewels and gold.*

*Until then, you must remember how I showed you how to be loving and tender.*

*I showed you how to be forgiving and kind. I showed you how to be giving without spending a dime.*

*While I was not perfect, I had some flaws you probably didn't see. That's simply because of Jesus who lived in me.*

*So, I suggest you get to know Him and accept Him for yourself. He's the only way you'll get to see me again. You can't come through anyone else.*

*Please don't wait too long to make up your mind.*

*Don't cry for me. I'm doing just fine.*

## Remember

*Although we prepare for the day to come, we're never really ready when it actually arrives.*

*Now that it has come and your physical presence is no longer here, we'll do our best to focus on all the memories we hold dear.*

*We'll remember the mischief, the laughter, and yes, even the tears. We've shared so very much through the years.*

*You lived a life of service. Your helping hands tended to others in need.*

*You loved not only with words but also in deed.*

You bravely fought each battle; one after the other they came.

Your battles are now over. You will no longer suffer pain.

And with each memory we share, there is joy in knowing your living was not in vain.

*M*y Auntie used to fuss because I never seemed to have aluminum foil and paper towels when she came over. The fact of the matter is I had simply learned to live without them.

## Without You

*My love for you has grown so much that you have become a necessary part of my every day. When you're not around, my skies are grey. Longing to have you near me, I try to occupy my time. But even that gets hard because you're constantly on my mind. Sometimes I wish that we could spend each moment of everyday wrapped in each other's arms. Yet I realize that isn't always possible because you have obligations, and so do I. We spend quite a bit of time together already. When it's time to part I never want to let you go. They say that absence makes the heart grow fonder. I know that to be true. I can hardly wait to see you again after being without you.*

*H*ave you ever not wanted to be first? Like when they ask for volunteers for group projects, are you an "eager beaver"? I almost never volunteer to go at all, let alone go first.

## From One First Born to Another

*I'm the first born. Yes, that's me.*

*While it does have its perks, it's not always what it's hyped up to be.*

*Growing up you get to "tell" the younger ones what to do.*

*But as you grow older you worry more about them too.*

*Sometimes you may have felt like the weight of the world was on your shoulder.*

*But do you remember when you could hardly wait to get older?*

*Well, how does it feel? You've finally arrived.*

*You've reached the three score and ten, for which so many strive.*

*I don't expect that you'll sit down somewhere and be still.*

*So, I wish you the very best as you travel the other side of the hill.*

*T*rying to find the right card for any occasion can sometimes be a daunting task. I mean, you could spend hours going through the various card selections only to learn that a handwritten note may have been the best action.

## Happy Valentine's Day!

*I wanted to send you a card to express how much you mean to me.*

*All of the cards I read had words that were sweet.*

*However, none of the words came close to describing the joy that loving you brings.*

*They were not the words to the melody my heart sings.*

*So, I decided to write this for you instead,*

*In hopes that it expresses more than any card you could have read.*

*I love you more today than I did yesterday, and tomorrow I'll love you even more.*

*The song my heart sings for you I've never heard before.*

*Sometimes it's hard to explain what it means to have you in my life.*

*You came along and loved me past the pain that was buried deep inside.*

*You're the reason my heart sings a love song.*

*I can't imagine how things would be had you not come along.*

*Now you're with me, and I pray you'll always stay*

*Because the love I have for you only grows stronger each day.*

*So, I pray that this expresses to you in some way*

*Just how much you mean to me.*

*I Love You!*

*Happy Valentine's Day!*

*C*ommunication rules the nation, or so I've heard. However, effective communication is key to success. It doesn't do any good if the communication isn't understood by all parties involved. Speak plainly. Say what you mean, and man what you say.

## Have I Told You

*Have I told you lately you mean the world to me?*

*Have I told you, "Thank you," for letting my love fly free?*

*Have I told you how wonderful you make me feel?*

*Have I told you how blessed I am for a love so real?*

*Have I told you that you're the spark that lights my fire?*

*Have I told you that your love is the heat of my burning desire?*

*Have I told you how I crave the taste of your kiss?*

*Have I told you how my body yearns for your caress?*

*Have I told you how much I miss you every moment you're away?*

*Have I told you that my love for you grows stronger every day?*

*Just in case I haven't told you, I want you to know*

*That the love and desire I have for you*

*Continue to grow and grow.*

*Just in case I haven't told you,*

*If you haven't got a clue,*

*Let me bring this rhyme to an end by saying*

*I love you.*

*W* hen we're dining out, I like to ask for a glass of water with "a twist" of lemon. Sounds fancy, doesn't it? Next time you order a glass of tea, water, or some other beverage of choice, ask for a twist of lemon, or lime even. Enjoy the experience.

## Heaven with a Twist

When I take all the passion, all the desire, all the love I have for you, mix them all together and seal it with a kiss,

I get a high I've never had before, and with each hit I fiend for more.

Addicted? Yes, I am. I can't remember a time I ever felt like this. How do I explain the high I get? Well, it's like heaven, "heaven with a twist".

Yes, heaven with a twist, that's what it is. There's no other way to describe the feeling this drug gives.

I remember the very first time I took a hit. I was so high that it scared me. I didn't want to get addicted, so I quit.

I thought I was doing pretty good. The urge to take another hit was being suppressed.

However, the urge grew stronger. I began to flirt with the desire that was building inside.

After a while though, I couldn't fight it any longer.

I took a hit.

Wow! This high was even better, no, scarier.

So, there I was, high as I wanted to be but afraid that I would get addicted. I knew I didn't want to go without it, but I didn't want to be dependent.

I began to get a few hits. One here. Another there. It wasn't on a regular basis. I thought, "I can handle this. Nothing to fear."

Yes, I handled it for a little while. That is until the urge began to grow.

You see, it not only satisfies physically. It even satisfies mentally and emotionally.

Stress relief, emotional stabilizer, mentally intriguing, body stimulating. All that wrapped in an attractive package. How could I resist? I don't doubt that others would like a hit of this.

When I think back on the progression of this addiction, I see nothing that I would have done differently. Always there, ready to satisfy whatever needed to be filled. Quenching a thirst that was unquenchable. All that I needed at all the right times. Even the right words and a few rhymes.

Why heaven, "heaven with a twist"? Well, I gave it some thought, and it just fits. Perfectly.

When I look up and see the vast blue sky, I know that heaven is beyond it. It symbolizes my high.

Whenever you're around, it's hard to let you go. It's not just the sexual satisfaction you bring. It's your realness, how we talk, how you make me laugh, personality, sensuality, all the stuff that makes you who you are. With all that combined and so much more, heaven is the only word big enough to contain it all.

Have you ever been high? A high so amazing you could cry? I have. Just when that high was at its highest height, it was sealed with a kiss. A kiss full of passion, oh my goodness, it was sweet. Like "coconut bliss". Yes! That's the twist.

I must be honest. I didn't come up with the name on my own. No, it isn't from any lyrics to a song.

I doubt that either of us at the time gave it much thought. You said, "Hey, Miss." "Hi," was my reply. Then you came back with, "You're like heaven with a twist. Sort of like coconut bliss."

Although it didn't at the time,

Now it makes perfect sense.

*P* uzzles are a wonderful tool for exercising the brain. There are so many different types of puzzles! I've recently grown fond of an app that requires you to figure out locks and puzzles that lead to another and then another until you open the main lock, and Voila!

## Picking up the pieces

A puzzle, that once fit together perfectly, rests crumbled in a pile of chaos and confusion. How can such a work of art be totally destroyed? Well, maybe 'totally destroyed' isn't the right description because that would be saying that it can't be repaired or put back together. Instead, it's been torn apart, broken to pieces. In an effort to restore the beauty that once was, the pile is scattered in order to sort through the pieces, putting aside the pieces that can't be easily placed. With all the edges gathered, the frame begins to smooth out giving some sense of direction on how to proceed. Once the edges are complete and intact, then and only then can the rest of the pieces be put in place. Within the walls formed by the edges, pieces are placed in their proper places; some forming smaller groups that can't yet be attached to the frame. Slowly, but surely, beauty starts to take form. As the puzzle is restored, the smaller groups are attached, and the remaining pieces are placed. After what seems like forever, the puzzle is once again complete. Amazingly the chaos and confusion that once was, has now become a clear picture. Unless the puzzle is untouchable, or out of reach, it's bound to be torn apart yet again only to be put back together, piece by piece. After going through the cycle, a number of times, the pieces become worn and don't fit as well as before. Nevertheless, they are all still pieces of the same puzzle and won't fit anywhere else. Amazingly, the puzzle's picture appears to have more character for the wear. Yet it is fragile, and more care must be taken to not 'totally destroy' even a single piece or else the puzzle will forever be incomplete.

*N*ow that all of my children are adults, I haven't bought a lot of Christmas gifts. I mean, shopping is my least favorite thing to do during the holidays. For those of you who love the hustle and bustle, shop friendly and be courteous to the workers.

## This Christmas

As we approach the Christmas holiday, let us not forget why we celebrate.

When you put up the tree so full and green, remember the life of the Newborn King. The evergreen tree is green all year long and never dies. Jesus is life. Did you not know He is indeed alive?

While putting up lights, so colorful and bright, can you imagine how glorious the angels must have looked to the shepherds that night? Maybe you should google images of the aurora lights.

The star that's placed atop the tree represents the guiding star that led the shepherds and the wise men three. The light of the world is Jesus Christ. Will you let him be your guiding light?

If exchanging gifts remember, they presented Him with special gifts that night. Have you *accepted the gift He gave? The gift of salvation, eternal life?*

*So, as we go through this holiday season, let us remember why we celebrate. Jesus is the reason for the season.*

*Wishing you a Merry Christmas and a Prosperous New Year*

*I*t's said that all good things must come to an end. This will complete the collage. We're near the end.

## This is How it Ends

*Well, here we are once again.*

*Back to square one where we first began.*

*I thought things would be different this time.*

*But to no avail, you started servin' the same ol' lines.*

*It seems that the chase is what gets you excited.*

*'Cause now that I'm the aggressor your flame is no longer ignited.*

*You tell me you love me more than your own life,*

*And one day you'd like to make me your wife.*

*I've contemplated the idea of you and me together,*

*But then I come to realize that, alone, my life is much better.*

*Don't get me wrong, your lovin' is the bomb.*

*However, there's more to life than sex, and that's where we went wrong.*

*It started with the late-night phone calls, askin' me if I was asleep.*

*Then it slowly escalated, and feelings started to grow deep.*

*Wanting to believe that all you said was true, I thought, "Maybe this time he'll stay."*

*When I tried to pull us closer, you began to pull away.*

*One minute, with me is where you want to spend all your free time.*

*The next minute, I'm left standing at the end of the line.*

*You say you admire me, the strength I exemplify as a single black mother.*

*You say how much you love me, and for you there is no other.*

*Unfortunately, I need much more than three simple words or mere admiration.*

*It seems the only time you're into me is when you feel the need for ejaculation.*

*Unlike other women you may have been with, it doesn't take the world to make me happy.*

*Nor is it all about the dolla's, for that I can get a suga' daddy.*

*I only ask for a few small things. One of them, understanding,*

*Is impossible for you to do when you want to be demanding.*

*I guess what I'm really trying to say is that I can't keep going on this way.*

*Going around in circles over and over. STOP! I'm getting off of this roller coaster.*

# Closing

I do hope you've had a wonderful time reading as I have had a joyful time writing and putting this collage together. ❤

# The End